Life Potions On Paper

one poem at a time

Orinthia

BookLeaf Publishing

India | USA | UK

Made with ❤ on the BookLeaf Publishing Platform
www.bookleafpub.in
www.bookleafpub.com

Dedication

This book is dedicated to a man who never stopped believing in me ! My Dad.

Preface

Welcome. If you're holding this book, it means a little piece of my heart has found its way into your hands. This collection of poems marks my first foray into sharing the scribbles of the last 15 years that have long echoed within me and in my diary.

Acknowledgements

To my family and friends, your unwavering belief in me and endless encouragement fueled this journey. Thank you for being my first and most steadfast audience.

1. The hunt

A thousand years ago I hunted you
A thousand times I have forgotten
A thousand miles I crossed for you
Only to honor the hunt.

The tale I tell is not a snowball
It is the fire that burns
It is the pumping heart
Who swallows the big chunks.

The traces are gone
The heads remain.
A silent army in my drawing room
As I sit by the window.

The fawn, the buck, the stag
A piece here on the southwest corner
A piece there behind the dining table
But I still look outside .

A quiet evening of light snow
Like it meant to reveal
A man who knows his way.
My aiming gun behind the pine trees.
As soon as it moved
A bullet went through and through
Like a nice touch of grey
The walls on the staircase
Just received a piece.

A piece of my heart,
A piece of my hunt.

2. A girl who knows

There was a girl in the woods
A little piece of life by the river
A dog, a cat, a few hens
Made a home for each other

She had the water from the river
And the green life on the shore
A little dark and a little smile
She was all that and much more

The tiger and his family
Were loyal to her
The pigs and the wolf
Loved her from afar.

It was the keep
The woods by the river
For the queen of the herd
There was no fear.

There was a little girl in the woods
Who lived and owned the land
The world never knew-
A girl who knows the land.

3. A lost world

A lot of sunshines later
There came the reaped happiness
The big stones fell from the sky
Like an evil God was to confess.

A trap was laid on earth
The waves made it easy
The washed away existence
Like a scene of forgotten fizzy.

The core was tight
Like a tough little child
It was the last to break
Slow and mild.

In the last piece of time
As all went back in the air
Ashes took the last stride
Like a dirt face filled with smear

A lost world was just here.

6

4. Writer's block

Fanny was a fat guy,
He ate a lot of cheese
Fanny had a full family
Who never were his.

Fanny had a pile of books
Some he read and some he wrote
Fanny had a closed door
The world was an invisible coat.

Fanny had a lot of time
He cried and prayed to all
A drop of thought, a hand of words
And Fanny would have it all.

Fanny had a lot of ink
A wooden table and a paper
Fanny kept staring at the ceiling
His unfinished story moved farther

Fanny was a thoughtful mind
Wrote the priest on wood
Fanny was our beloved
Said the priest with a mood
Fanny left a white paper
Before he left this world for good.

5. Macbeth has no regret

It is when you hammer the belief
A scarlet mind can understand
Only if he could walk away
Ousting the witches' foretell by the hand
Let's reckon a world where he has.
A general as fiery as him,
He served his domain,
And never felt any grim.

What if he spilled no blood
A clean white collar
What if he can never be bribed
Not even the kingship
Not interested in any leap
What if he just lived
A man planting trees
He knows will outgrow him.

A Scottish life lived in quiet
What if he could be happy

A margined destiny
Crafted inside the border.
Could all the greatness be besieged
Could the goodness be then met
It is then he would become Macbeth
A man who has no regret.

6. A nice cup of tea

In the middle of the day
In the last minute of each hour
As the clock runs the day
As Batman falls from the tv stand
And the greasy bowl stands in between
A haste that fills the last hour
Hour before tommy's kitchen show
Just after the peaceful nap
And the call of the azaan
Just in time for a sandal incense stick.

What brings the joy
The joy of an adroit evening
Filled with sunset and breeze
What takes away the heart
Like the first song of the infant
Like a rose garden from the mountains
And the comfort of a life
So familiar that calls a home

A home that is called
A nice cup of tea.

12

7. Changer

And then they met…
The sand slipped through the beautiful sun masked
morning,
Dismissing the line of friendship and love into a distant
invisible.
There are so many miracles in the world for eyes to
behold,
Like the two of them completely distracted
With too much smothering closeness.

To him, she's a little bit of magic
And to her,
He is a stirring blend of disobedience and deep thoughts.

Gazing into each other's depths, they were changed
forever.

8. Birds of the same flock

She was heard from a distance
Like a beautiful summer day.

She could be seen on the porch
Quiet, like an old closed book.

She was the colored dandelion
In a happy sunny backyard.

She was the honest apple pie
Waiting to be engulfed.

She was Daddy 's pride
His hero in his life

She was Mom's whole heart
An emotional swiss knife.

A piece here, a piece there
Such is the haste of God.

One had eyes and one had tongue
Born like two peas in a pod.

15

9. Sailors' excursion

And through the torrid winds of the chilled evening
storm,
They sailed without a stop, they backspaced themselves
Only to write again, only to anchor again,
Even at a distance, even at an edge-
Flying together at the dark blue and the ivory alike
Only to be found again, and again...
In the small space away from the world
They were found holding each other
Even through the tempered winds they sailed.
Laughing and living as the chapters unfold slowly.

10. Stolen

Are you blind to the pain ?
An angry husband roared
Ending the routine beatings

Are you not in your senses ?
An innocent son looked up
Holding her mother close

Is this how the evening should look ?
She removed the hair on her face
A groping smile had taken over her.

A little bit of devil,
A little bit of ice cream
Her eyes rose to the occasion

Just a few hours back
From what she became a girl
A renewed youth in her big eyes

Just a few hours back
A love from the past
Like a ghost, he was
He who had stolen
A few good glances
To last her a bunch of evenings.

11. Draft of freedom

He rode and rode,
Till the sand erode-
To drop a note to self.

It was the note-
The note was found,
To set a chain on fire.

It was the fire-
its plight and pain,
To gain a sight of self.

It was the note -
The note was key,
To carve a draft of freedom.

12. Black

"I can't see…. I can't see anything, son"
The anxious old voice circled the hospital dorm.

"We have to take her home, I have decided, its done."
Said the son to his nonchalant wife.

It has been five years she missed home.
She thanked God, for trading color for the comforting
black.

13. A beautiful mistake

It was in the air
A deep cold sense
It was in the snow
A sacred white secret
What a lovely Christmas eve !

On the pavement
There sat a girl
With big asking eyes
Like a blot of blue ink
On the white snow paper.

I stopped at her,
I met with her at ease
There was a game of coins
Like the god's honest truth
She and I began to play.

The heads you win,
The tails you lose.

It was simple.
Round after round
I lost a lot of hands.

Out in the world
Life's a bland pale soup
This little play was the truth.
As I let her win,
Not in any fear
But I reeled a lot

I lived a little
I breathed a little
For this beautiful mistake.

14. Cancer

He laughed at his own expense
He danced at his own mistakes.
He made every day mundane into conceivable amazing.

Every day he went home with little less life.
Cancer was just a name.

15. Gone with the wind

The end of the world doesn't feel like the end of the
world at all.
It feels different.
You can see the farewell breaths going out of you.
The pale blue and white coloured soul coming out of you
and straight into the ocean.

It will dissolve.

It gives the feeling that your entire existence is
dissolving into thin air, into a mix of nothing and
everything.
All the hand holding and all the slow whispers reverses
itself to the very beginning.
And for the last time everything appears in full bloom,
the colours are so prominent for once and then it's gone.

Just like that, it isn't there anymore.

The good ,bad and ugly, everything is gone with the
wind.

25

16. Fire

A theoretical life was over
As over as it could be
There was grey and the black
The burning red for all to see.

The ladder man took him out
He was under the desk
His books and bed
Became a imagery, grotesque.

All the love in this world
It was taken
A moment's notice
Should have been given

His cars, and stars
Like a black cinema.
His dog , Lava
And the grandma.

He lived through all
All that he lost
And stared at the scene
A fire that he did start.

17. The pleasure and pains of coffee

Is it the smell, the absolutely unabated breath of morning freshness peeping through the cup's brim which gets you started;
It can also be the sudden rush to get things moving in your otherwise slightly peevish, slightly turtle-like 9ams. My mom used to despise excessive use of caffeine but it was quite easily nullified as I sat with my grandfather, in our own spirited chumminess, to enjoy the morning coffee.

I was not addicted. I was captivated.

When bad hair days' pop up out of nowhere and you just strive to make it to the finishing line, then something pulls you out, in a sprightly manner from all that was stuck. It helps you to get over the spilled milk and still have a smile on your face.

It's like the coffee makes a grand entry in you, and ideas

begin to move like the true-blue unfailing army of the
Grandest battle ever unveiling all that was promised to
be treated very gingerly.

With coffee, things remembered arrive at full gallop.

18. The Sun

The sun is at the centre of everything.
The hue and burns in the most ineffective filters of the
universe.

Like you come too close,
You scorch out into nothing,

You stay away
You senile yourself into a blend of minimum and merely.

The list of everything necessary and everything
damaging...
All my complete, to all my core breaking points
Straight Lined into six feet of happy horizon.

There he stands, my life in front of my life.

19. Farewell

She didn't know what to feel...
She felt empty.
She emptied her reserved spirit into thankless glasses
Which failed to contain her overflow.

She may have spread herself to many,
But the stage was her playfield.
She chose the crowded stage over the togetherness.
She chose the backstage chaos and incoherence
Over calm and candle lights.

She earned it.

All the pain and all the glory.
It was all hers and hers only.
Tomorrow will be her last show.

They signed the papers.
They put up dutiful farewell glances all week.
They arranged for her way out.

20. Definition of love

For when you do the thing
The thing that tings
Like a dry rose inside an old book
Like is a surprise midnight snack

For when you peep through the window
The wait is what you crave
Like a hot mothers' meal
Like the smell of a dear old grandma

For when you seek more in hide and seek
Willing to bear your soul
Like a beautiful testimony
Like a sunset at a mountain top

Is that when you are in love ?
Is that what it feels like ?
The shiny red ribbon -
Waiting to be born.

Is that how love is?
A teenage soul scribbling about life.
For the first time on paper,
Leaving a sacred fragment of her
On the pages of this dairy.

For when you open the door,
You let the light in ;
And never become anything
Other than your heart
On this day.
As pure as a candle on Christmas eve.

21. The most simple thing

And when everything becomes dull, then I look at
myself.
Sitting beside me, wrapping hands around my shoulder ,
Oozing a peaceful exuberance .

The other me, she is a far superior being than my petty
self.
There are no effects of any external happenings on her
face.
All that is present is a calm reflection of the within.
She almost had a Monalisa smile.

In these times, I dare not to look at this face of hers.
The quiet that comes out of her is a supremely strong
radiation.
My tangled neurons feel fumbled and fear in front of this
force.
The force that skillfully absorbs all the crooked dark and
reflects only on the clear blue sky.

The tear ducts feel sleepy in front of this other me
As if they had sniffed a poignant flower and fallen into
Rip Van Winkle's dream sequence.

In short, I feel pretty powerless in front of her.
To my surprise, all the luggage is on my side.
Just next to me there is the box full of my unfulfilled
dreams,
Then on my right there are a bunch of emotions nicely
tied with a rubber band. Then on both my hands I have
two heavy bags of words of unkind people .
Finally on my lap is the slimy bag of regret that keeps its
movement
Just Like the uninvited cat during meal time.

All that defines me are on my side and there she sits,
The other me ,of course without any luggage.
When I look at her , she smiles at my surprise
And like the intelligent detective indicates towards her
mind.

Now what does that mean,
These luggages are all inside her mind? Really?
Then how is she so happy. I asked her?
Is this a pretense?
This calm that you have,
Like the strongest storm can touch you

And still you will remain the same.

To this, she again indicated her mind.
This time like a weapon.
I think she wanted to tell me
That her mind is her biggest weapon.

There was no necessity in her,
Necessity to fight, to win, to cry
Or even to express.
She sat there, breathing, like a ray of hope
Like the most simple thing in the world.